Walking on the Boundaries of Change

Poems of Transition by
SARA HOLBROOK

KID POEMS FOR THE NOT-SO-BAD
Cleveland, OH

This book is dedicated to
Dee
for answering all of those calls at 3 a.m.

Many thanks and accolades to:

Kathleen Traynor and Kelly Traynor
editorial assistance

Martin Reuben Photography
cover design, photography and art

Leslie Krupman
graphic design and typesetting

Herwell Press
printing

ISBN: 1-881786-10-2

KID POEMS FOR THE NOT-SO-BAD
P. O. Box 40084
Cleveland, OH 44140

Contents

REAL FRIENDS

Day by day
a tightrope,
walking on the boundaries
of change.
One step —
firm, familiar,
the next step —
shaky, strange.
Some friends
will dare danger,
mock or push each step.
Some friends
knock your confidence.
Real friends
form a net.

A DIFFERENT FIT

Sometimes
I feel so different —
a maple leaf
turned red in June,
displaying colors I can't quiet,
about as subtle
as a sonic boom.

Today,
I want to fit in,
another speck in the sparrow crowd.
Not be perched like an ostrich in hiding
with embarrassing parts sticking out.

Why can't I gravel-crunch along
with all the rest of the rocks
instead of feeling like an alien
standing out
in neon socks?

THE STORM THAT WAS

Me?
I rolled in like a storm,
darkening the room,
ominously rumbling,
then erupting with a BOOM!

I HATE PEOPLE.
I HATE SCHOOL.
I HATE WHAT'S HOT.
I HATE WHAT'S COOL.
I CAN'T STAND RIDING BUSES.
ALL MY FRIENDS ARE MEAN.
THE WORLD IS GUACAMOLE
AND
I HATE THE COLOR GREEN.

And you?
You didn't run for cover,
or have that much to say.
You listened to my cloudburst.

And the storm?
It blew away.

TIME FOR RECESS?

I need an outdoor recess –
inner mood swings,
make my mental hands wring
and poke my face into this pout.
I'm counting seconds –
where's the bell?
I need to run and scream and shout.
I'm all tied up inside.
This is serious.
Let me out!

A NICE TRIP?

If I bumble-bump along,
clutz-awkward,
like some sloth-toed-gangle-geek...

If I stupid-stumble slip
or free-fall flat
from foolish, flappy feet ...

If I trip
or just get stuck knee-deep in
quick-set doubt...

I know I may look dumb.
But
do you have to point that out?

ACTING SPOOKY

This time not a headless horseman,
haunted castle or vampire's coffin.
It's not midnight or Halloween.
There's no face in the window
or ghoulish fiend
hiding underneath the bed.
This time the spooks
are in my head.

Am I crazy?
Am I confused?
Are they talking about me?
Have I been used?

Imagination can make me scared,
when I see things that are not there.
Do I look like a fool?
Have I been put-down?
The ghosts in my head
start flying around.

Before I jump out a window
or act like I feel.
STOP!
I need to be
checking out
just what is real.

SLIPPED

I slipped.
Everything seems to stink.
I better
check my shoe.
I can't tell
where or when
but, yes,
I guess,
I stepped in a rotten mood.

SELF ESTEEM?

I tell my dog he's bad.
I laugh when he jumps and misses.
I gag when he drinks from the toilet
and then tries to give me kisses.
I mock the way he twitches his nose
and sometimes he makes me scream.
His nicknames are
"stinky" and "hairball."
Can dogs get low self-esteem?

A REAL CASE

Doubtful I have a fever
or any other measurable symptom.
I'm just down with a sniffily case
of sudden-self-loathing-syndrome.

TODAY!
It hit like a thwop of mashed potatoes
snapped against a plate,
an unrequested extra serving
of just-for-now-self-hate.

Today, I feel worthless,
a left-over bath,
a wad of second-hand gum.
I belong in a twist-tied bag
with the rest of the toys that won't run.

My mood's as welcome as
incoming dog breath,
or a terminal case of split ends.
I sparkle like a dust rag,
I could attract mosquitoes −
maybe − not friends.

In fact, I could be contagious!
I'm a downer to say the least.
And if you try and push
my mood swing,
I'll probably drag my feet.

Why?
I couldn't tell you.
Some days,
I get up and get down.
It's not a permanent disability, though.
Tomorrow,
I'll come around.

HAPPY ALL AROUND

Happy settles,
an orange campfire in my chest.
Peaceful,
not a scattering wildfire
quickly covering ground.
A slow glow,
my inner circle,
warm,
attracting others all around.

CAN WE BE FRIENDS?

I have had an overview
of little bits
of all of you.
I circle for a place to land.
Trying to find the best approach,
looking casual,
unplanned.
I'm not up for showing off
and I don't want to pretend.
No high-flying acrobatics –
I just want to be your friend.

CONFIDENTIALLY SPEAKING

We don't advertise
our friendship,
or billboard all the fun we had.
I offer you a put-down,
"Chump!"
And you return a jab,
"Fool!"
We're not for looking sissy.
We strike and spark,
but don't explode.
We're talking highly confidential –
a dot-dash-Morse-code.
We poke.
We shove.
We jerk around
and no one can suspect
that when we push away,
for a moment
we connect.

A CHOICE

You can scold
or we can converse.
We can talk,
or we can curse.
We can form a team
or fight to be first...
but not both.

I can ask
or I can demand.
I can shake my fist
or shake your hand.
We can walk together
or take a stand...
but not both.

A state of mind,
a tone of voice.
Confrontation — cooperation,
a personal choice.
One or the other...
but not both.

VIOLENCE HURTS

Flailing fists can be one solution,
one way to conflict resolution.
So's an insult.
So's a gun.
We could fight to the death,
get vengeance obsessed,
or strike like a hit and run.

Or we could huddle on neutral ground,
pass a few words around.
For once,
we could see if just talking works.
Maybe settle this.

Violence hurts.

LEAVING MESSAGES

I talked to Mary-Virginia.
I talked to Paulie.
I talked to the check-out guy
at the store.
I talked to Beronica,
about 100 times,
but I needed to talk some more.

So I talked to opposing teams
when we took a drink at halftime.
I called in on the radio
and talked to the
Aluminum-Siding-Help-Line.

I talked to my journal.
I talked to Mitch
every other Tuesday,
which
didn't help.
Nothing helped.
I couldn't get the message through
until
I bit my lip
and finally talked to you.

BETTER THAN?

The snob
hides behind
a designer exterior
putting down others
and acting superior.

He's
the smoothest,
the richest,
most likely to win.
Which he'll tell you
before
you can even ask him.

He's
constantly buffing
his wax of perfection.
He shines
from a distance
but
not
on
closer inspection.

RUMORS

Garbage in.
Garbage out.
The rumor input trail,
one story in the database
and the news is in the mail.

The facts get gobbled byte by byte
as the fiction is repeated,
spreading like a virus.
The truth,
once crowded from the memory,
is automatically deleted.

DISAPPOINTMENT

Disappointment!
What a surprise.
You're a blast from door's-open-cold.
You're nuts in my chocolate cream.
You're a late lunch
and bread sprouting mold.

Disappointment?
You're a blister
from new favorite shoes.
You promised and then you forgot.
You're just crumbs
where there once was a cake.
You looked honest,
but then you were not.

Disappointment.
You took pliers and yanked out my trust
like a dentist without novocaine.
Then you didn't return my calls
when I tried to express my pain.

RECYCLING CENTER

Gloria's good at – other people's.
Other people's habits.
Other people's dress.
Other people's relationships.
Her stuff just sits there and collects.
She sorts through
other people's garbage
and ignores her rotting stash.
It's stinky,
how she just keeps recycling
other people's trash.

TEAMMATES

A friendship should
have checkups:
pressures,
weights,
temperatures (hot and cold),
before it overextends,
gets sick,
or breaks
for separate goals.

THE HEART OF FRIENDSHIP

We shake hands
and touch
the heart of friendship,
you and I,
with halting eyes,
a brief exchange
of lips and then
good-bye.
You leave your thanks
and honest laugh,
no questions,
why do I
seem to have
one more reply?

JUST IMAGINE

Loves me...
Loves me not...
Loves me...
Loves me not...
The petal popping,
forehead bopping,
heartbeat stopping
question leaves me
sometimes singing,
then eyeballs stinging,
both hands wringing
crazy.
Is it love?
How can I know?
Just imagine
if it were so.
I'd be calm,
since I would know.
Love, not craziness
would grow.
Just imagine
if it were so.
Just imagine
if it were so.
Just imagine if it were so!
Ah...

HOMECOMING

Look here.
I'm talking football.
And you?
You're talking dance.
I hope we cream the Bears.
You're looking for romance.
I say we give it up.
We're like a mustard-jelly sandwich.
Homecoming?
You kidding?
You don't even speak my language.

A STEP

Two,
awkward about the front door,
fiddling with good-bye.
Too close for a wave or a handshake.
Too close.
Too far.
Too shy.

A step in the dark...
would it be an intrusion?
Would it ruin a friendship?
Cause conflict?
Confusion?

Two,
poised on that risky step,
not quite eye-to-eye,
searching for the right key
to get them through
good-bye.

NEEDY CAT

She nuzzles up,
head begging
for a loving pat,
then turns away,
soft purring,
without looking back.
Pretending independence,
that needy little cat.

A love
is what she wants.
Aloof
is what you see.
I'd probably ignore her
if she weren't
a lot like me.

FAST LOVE

Kissing Kristin's popular.
Real popular,
with boys.
A presidential candidate
would like
the fame that she enjoys.

It isn't 'cause she's beautiful,
talented or smart.
She's just fast
and user friendly
like a quick-stop-dairy-mart.

Fast love
is like fast food.
Sometimes it *looks*
delicious.
But, it doesn't satisfy
because
it isn't that nutritious.

Kristin's not so bad,
she's on these food runs
all alone.
Trying to pick up
what's out-of-stock
at home.

GET IT IN GEAR

If love is a go,
trust is first gear.
Shift into threats,
lies or fear...
Bam!
You drop the transmission.

Love's out of commission.

THE LAKE

To know it,
moodily changing,
constant and same.
To understand it,
black-eyed and brooding,
unfurrowed and tame.
Loving its smell,
to be drawn to its shore.
To look,
to look,
to see and want more.
Direction uncertain,
to ride it bareback.
And never to question,
does it love back.

AFFECTION OBJECTION

Two,
velcroed together,
not...you know...
but close.
Love by the lockers
is gooey-gone-gross.
I've a pretty high tolerance
for public affection,
but, hey,
this kind of romance
calls for public objection.
Who are you,
Lewis and Clark?
You want to explore?
Then take it outside.
Please.
This scene is hard core.
This hallway's not zoned
for lip locks, hip locks
or going-to-town.
Take a breath.
Lighten up.
Look,
there're freshmen around.

MIDNIGHT

When it's Sunday
and it's midnight,
the weekend
put back in its chest,
the toys of recreation,
party times and needed rest...

When I lay in wait
for Monday
to grab me by the ear,
throw me at the shower,
off to school...
And when I hear
the train at midnight
from so many miles away...
When it's Sunday...
And it's midnight...
the train
in passing brays and boasts
it's steel-track-straight,
on schedule,
arrival times to keep.
I meander to it's rhythm,
flopping like a fish.
Why can't I get to sleep?
Why can't I get to sleep?

UNTIL

It was nothing,
never mentioned
at dinners
and pass the tension.
Lips together
politely chewing,
not that tough,
a common stewing.
Never solved,
the problem
swallowed,
not resolved.
Each dinner balanced
by strength of will.
The family excused,
almost,
until...

WHO DID?

Stop! Halt!
My fault? My fault?
Your fault. Your fault.
Your fault. Your fault.

Who let anger in the house
to drop its bitter litter everywhere,
causing us to stumble, grumble,
slip and trip and glare?
You did. He did?
I did? She did.
You did. You did.
You did. You did.

It took over in a snap.
Who said anger was the boss?
Now, we're up to here in grudges.
Someone tell it to get lost.
I should? I should?
He should. She should.
You should. You should.
You should. You should.

Oh, forget who let the anger in.
Blame games get so mean.
This mess is getting out of hand.
How 'bout, we all pitch in and clean.

PART OF THE JOB
DESCRIPTION

Nature gives us a mother
to fry our chicken,
shrink our sweatshirts
and spoil our fun.
But like pillows,
it's a pain in the neck to
have to juggle more than one.
It's her job to ask me to explain
where I was
and what I did.
It's not your job,
it's hers,
to make me
feel like a little kid.

HEAR IT?

I don't want to talk about *it.*
It's secret.
You wouldn't believe *it* anyway.
I'm locked.
I lost the key.
It doesn't matter what we say.
Nothing will change.
It's not that bad.
It doesn't bother me a bit.
It's my problem, anyway
and I can handle *it.*
It's a private hand I have to play.
It's about cards I cannot show.
It doesn't matter.
Go away.
It would be wrong for you to know.
I should have stopped *it* long ago.
I'm serious.
Leave me alone.
You can't understand *it*
or my fear.
Get out.
I have nothing to say.
Don't you get *it* ?
Can't you hear?

RUN AWAY

I saw JoLynn just once
after she ran away.
We hugged at each other's eyes
and touched hands
but had little to say.

She said she was doing fine
except she lost her toothbrush.
She said she was better off
and I left wondering what the truth was.

She left family, control,
anger and arguments at home,
left lugging a stubborn suitcase
she has to carry all alone.

When she was running into
all those problems
she used to snap and spit
like fire.
But, now that she's run away,
the heat is off—
she just looks tired.

JUST SAY NO?

Slogans work
on billboards.
They don't meet
the kids I meet,
honking from the fast lane
down here on the street

No! might sound just like a put-down,
might attract too much attention.
No! might even spark a fight or
could ignite somebody's tension.

Just No can be a speech.
I'm better off with my own words,
finding my own way
to make myself be heard.

FOR REAL

This time
not a movie,
a song or a play.
This time
this kid
can't be scripted away.
He's here,
performing his pusher act.
I can't nice-nice
or not react.

This time
his sales pitch
in my face,
'til it's
standing-room-only
in my personal space.

This time,
my time
to say
goodnight,
turn my back
and
exit right.

PRIVATE PROPERTY

It's my body,
my choice,
what food I put inside.
What I wrap around me.
What I show
and
what I hide.
I'm not a public trash can,
a public road,
a public beach.
Public is for others.
Me?
I'm private property.

THE GUN

I'm smarter,
stronger,
faster,
unless you have the gun.

I have pride
and self-esteem,
my stuff —
unless you have the gun.

You disrespect my freedom,
friends can't hold
both guns and hands.
You don't even have to shoot
before
you've ripped off who I am.

BLOWN AWAY

There was never a rep like Tony's.
His was the coldest in the school.
In the library?
Check it out.
His picture's under cool.
He was exclusive,
an original,
we copied him
from his hair down to his stroll.
That was,
till Tony joined the Lizards
and the gang ate Tony whole.
Now, he wears their look,
their jacket,
their shoes,
their hat
and their tattoos.
He must have tossed his brain in the dumpster.
He even wears their attitudes.
The Lizards
tell him where to go,
who to talk to,
what to say.
Tony better get a grip
before he's blown away.

HIGH COST - LOW PRICE

Everywhere
inflation,
goods and prices
up and up,
except
the price on life
where
a rock
of crack
costs seven bucks.

MEANT TO BE FUN

It was just for fun —
a game of truth or dare.
No one meant to hurt.
No one meant to get so scared.

A game without a box,
a lid,
a single rule.
No one meant to dare real danger.
No one meant to be so cruel.

A game.
It was just for fun —
truth or dare,
we each could choose.
No one meant it.
Who could know —
that all of us would lose.

FINALS

The accident.
The news.
Sped like a lighted fuse
to dynamite
our homeroom.
Facts were scattered
and confused.
Who was driving?
At what speed?
What road?
What curve?
What time?
How bad?
Oh, god.
Which tree?
Respirator. Coma.
Lifeflight. CPR.
Today's vocabulary words,
new adjectives
for "car."
The explosion left us staring,
unresponsive
with fixed eyes,
at that blasted empty desk.
No retakes.
No good-byes.

GOOD GRIEF?

Grief gets worn out by grieving,
pain's a coat I must put on
and wear around the house
till it no longer feels so wrong.
I can't leave it in the box
and claim it doesn't fit.
I can't bag it for the coat drive
or wait
till I grow into it.
Not a color of my choosing
and nothing to brag about.
The sooner
I try grief on,
the sooner
the grief
will get worn out.

WHAT'S REAL?

Pictured between reruns
and what commercials want to sell,
explodes another war
in some far place
that I can't spell.

To me,
war appears as broken bodies,
burning buildings,
and smoking gas,
interrupted by auto salesmen,
frosty colas
and kitchen wax.

Every evening
around dinner
devastation,
served up with my meal,
is sprinkled with laundry powder.
It's hard to tell
which pictures are real.

FAST CHUCK

No one said Chuckie
didn't have brains,
to him learning and talking came fast.
Whether reading or rapping or math,
his ideas shot like fired rocket blasts.

He grabbed at new thoughts
like free candy,
never too much or enough.
He always had to be first,
even first learning all the wrong stuff.

Streetwise?
Now figuring angles
to get what his body
won't need, he is using
to keep himself going
on a desperate drive to succeed.

Fast Chuck.
Just racing to crash.
Skinny and jumpy with shakes,
his body is falling apart.
A rocket in a raggedy car,
a blast of fast, but how far?

SCREAM BLOODY MURDER?

When I see bodies on the news
it makes me want to cry all night.
'Course even if I do
it doesn't bring them
back to life.

What's the use in caring?
Can't we just pretend?
That everyone is nice –
and that all lives have happy ends?

If I turn my back to horror
or hum and close my eyes.
If I just refuse to see,
does it mean
those wronged
died twice?

REMEMBER?

I don't remember the first time,
how it started,
or when.
But I remember
the night you brought me brownies
and said
it would never happen again.

I remember
your hair was longer then
and how your eyes swam over to mine.
I remember
how my smile stuck on my teeth.
I knew it wasn't the last time.

My eyes were sealed with tears
and it was hard for them to wake,
but that didn't seem to matter.
We hugged.
And the brownies tasted great.

OLD PICTURES

See that hole in my smile
and the pat on my head?
I was so old
I could make my own bed.

I could find my own boots
and zipper my coat,
pick up my toys
and tie my own bows.

I am much older
since I lost that tooth,
but you want to know
the honest-to-truth?

Grown-up gets scary,
and that is a fact.
Where was my brain?
I should have
put that tooth back.

OVER THE LIMIT

LATE!
A panic fills my chest
and no space left to breathe.
HURRY! Tap-tap-LATE!
and why'd I wait so LATE! to leave?

LATE!
I really thought I had
a bulging pocket-full-of-time,
plenty left to spend,
until I looked up at the clock,
and saw the world was about to end.

LATE!
Just great.
How can I ever maintain credit
if I overspend my time,
a chronic repeat offender
addicted to the tardy crime?

I've got to learn my limit,
it hurts to function with no breath.
Got to break the habit.
Why do I cause me so much stress?

ARE YOU THE ONE?

No games today,
it's just into the bleachers
assembled for hearing
our principal preachers—

No smoking
No guns.
No drugs and
No fights.
No harassment of females.
No whites against blacks
No blacks against whites.

Eyes rolled to the rafters,
half-listening through
shoe-squeaks and pokes
we slouch.
Except for Priscilla,
and (naturally),
she's taking notes.

Consequences:
Demerits.
Detentions.
Suspensions.

Outlined
by some names,
of those who have laid out
the maximum fine for
flipping-off rules.
Those who've paid with their lives.
Each year,
they are telling us,
somebody dies.

What a waste.
What a bore.
We couldn't care less.
What a joke.
We leave.
We laugh—
and we guess . . .

Are you the one?

CREATIVE GRADES

Creative does,
'though not what's told,
a student
who is not enrolled
in graduated, chaptered classes,
where mindful competition passes
for excellence.
His recompense
is not achieved
by others brandishing respect.
Creative
grades its own neglect.

HOME AND AWAY

Sleep's my friend,
left warm-a-bed
while I'm to school
to fill my head
with haunting bone-pile histories,
algebraic mysteries,
and other take home tests
which I drag back to my nest.
Thoughts wrestle with Sleep,
they pillow fight,
their combat can
keep me up all night.

TO WIN

I really don't want to lose.
It's not
I've never lost before.
I did and did
and did,
and still came back
for more.

I know
that all good sports
learn how to win or lose
and not break stride.
That I can recycle pride.
That lost can play again.
That losing isn't a sin.

But...but
this time I want to win.

WHY DO SQUIRRELS CROSS THE ROAD?

I stopped to ask a
squirrel
about a fact
that's little known,
a silent eyeball chat.
No one was looking,
we were alone.

Branched out in that tree,
sniffing at the breeze,
he let me come this close
and count
his whiskers and his toes.

I asked,
"Squirrels climb and chase
all 'round the place,
bossing as they go.
But some
squirrels at play
get blown away.
Why *do* squirrels cross the road?"

He stretched
to point his nose at me,
so small,
his hands locked in
a starting block of tree.

"What are you, crazy?
Curious?
Bored?"
I asked,
"Are you nut-starved
or just lost your senses?
Wouldn't you be better off
fed and secure
behind some fences?
We could keep you safe..."

He stared his
black beads
straight at me.
Winked.
And off he raced.

IT'S ME, GOING PLACES

Day
meets Darkness,
corner of Dusk and Dawn.
They scratch and they yawn
with familiar faces
before shaking hands
and trading places.
I'm asleep
until the alarm
pistol-starts
my washing and brushing,
running laps of
bedroom to bathroom to bedroom,
strip, dress and flushing.
No time to sigh
as a tired mirror faces
my sleepy-eyed
fumbling with
buttons and laces.
Days aren't born busy,
it's me,
going places.
Day arrives calm.
Me?
I'm off to the races.

ACCOUNTING FOR FRIENDS

Security
is a bank account
I keep inside my mind.
Friends can make deposits
to be returned,
in kind.
You like my smile?
My thoughts?
My heart?
I stash your words away,
and when I'm low,
I make withdrawals
to help me feel okay.

I like your honesty?
Ideas?
The choices that you make?
I say the words,
contributing
to our friendly give-and-take.

Friendship — an investment,
where kindness is repaid,
accumulating interest
in trust for future trade.

ON THE RISE

Everybody's changing,
it isn't like first grade,
we hung those valentines on the wall,
our hearts looked similar,
displayed.
When we all stood to take the pledge,
we traveled in a line,
held two fingers up for quiet,
returned from recess,
every time.

Now, we all have different
destinations,
each our own speed,
each our own track.
Some seem lost
in the transition.
Can't go forward.
Can't go back.

We seemed more the same,
although
they told us we were different back then.
Little, multicolored snowflakes,
separating
when we rose up in a swirl
against brick buildings,
we rebelled.
Snowflakes.
No one told us.
Who would settle?
Who would fly?
and who
(and who?)
would melt?

LOSING IT

I must have lost a hundred pens.
I've lost my wallet.
I've lost my watch.
I can never find two slippers,
two sneakers or two socks.

I have a box of single gloves.
I've lost notebooks, papers, glasses.
I've lost pictures, sets of keys,
and two birthday movie passes.

I've lost stuff on the bus,
on my own, even on purpose.
I've lost soap down the drain
and lost my copy of *Red Badge of Courage.*
I never have more than 51 cards –
so I am not discouraged.

If I can lose both my change and the movie
just walking home from the video mart,
then I can lose this case of hatred
that's strangling my heart.

ON THE VERGE

Look inside this block of marble —
see the angle of a chin?
See? This part juts out —
and here?
It slopes back in?

I know it's just a block of marble —
but see the profile?
Use the light.
A shoulder, outstretched arm,
it's stepping forward.
Am I right?

Museum walls are lined
with graceful statues,
polished rocks,
smoothed of all their edges.
Works of art
that once were blocks like this.
Look here, a foot,
a hand, a nose,
an outline on the verge,
struggling to be seen.
A profile
trying to emerge.

OTHER BOOKS BY
SARA HOLBROOK

FEELINGS MAKE ME REAL

SOME FAMILIES

THE DOG ATE MY HOMEWORK

I NEVER SAID I WASN'T DIFFICULT

NOTHING'S THE END OF THE WORLD